Crafts to Make in the Summer

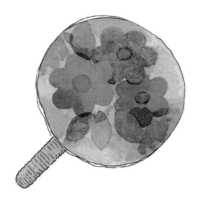

CRAFTS FOR ALL SEASONS

Crafts
to make
in the
Summer

KATHY ROSS

illustrated by Vicky Enright

The Millbrook Press   Brookfield, Connecticut

For my longtime friends, Sandy and Rema—K.R.

In memory of my sister Claudia, who loved the summer—V.E.

Library of Congress Cataloging-in-Publication Data
Ross, Kathy (Katharine Reynolds), 1948—
Crafts to make in the summer / Kathy Ross; illustrated by Vicky Enright.
p. cm. — (Crafts for all seasons)
Summary: Presents twenty-nine easy-to-make craft projects with summertime
themes, including a mouse sunglasses case, a firecracker finger puppet, and a
seashell candle holder.
ISBN 0-7613-0317-0 (lib. bdg.). —ISBN 0-7613-0334-0 (pbk.)
1. Handicraft—Juvenile literature. [1. Handicraft. 2. Summer.]
I. Enright, Vicky, ill. II. Title. III. Series: Ross, Kathy (Katharine Reynolds),
1948— Crafts for all seasons.
TT160.R714229 1998
745.5—dc21 97-25455 CIP AC

Published by The Millbrook Press, Inc.
2 Old New Milford Road
Brookfield, Connecticut 06804

Contents

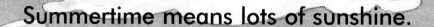

Talking Sun Puppet

Here is what you need:

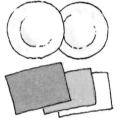 two 9-inch (23-cm) paper plates

 orange, yellow, and white construction paper

 yellow paint

paintbrush

aluminum foil

white glue

 scissors

yellow yarn

cardboard paper towel tube

black marker

pencil

newspaper to work on

two paper fasteners

rubberband (red one if possible)

Here is what you do:

1 Trace your hand on the colored paper. You will need to cut out five yellow hand shapes and six orange hand shapes.

2 Paint the bottom of one paper plate yellow.

3 Cover the bottom of the second plate with glue. Arrange the hand shapes around the edge of the gluey plate for the rays of the sun. Start and end with an orange hand, leaving a 2-inch (5-cm) opening between them where no hand "ray" sticks out.

5-

6-

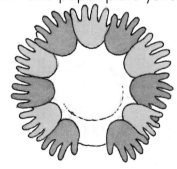

4 Set the top of the painted plate over the gluey plate so that you have a yellow sun with rays all around it. The opening will be the bottom.

5 To make the mouth, push the two paper fasteners into the sun above the opening and about 3 inches (8 cm) apart. Hook an end of the rubberband over each fastener. Open the fasteners on the back of the sun to secure them.

6 Cut two eyes from the white paper. Use the black marker to draw a pupil on each eye. Glue the eyes to the face of the sun.

7 Cover the cardboard tube with aluminum foil. Fold the extra foil down into the two ends of the tube. Cut a 2-inch (5-cm) slit on each side of the opening at one end of the tube. Slide the bottom edge of the sun into the slit.

8 Tie one end of a 24-inch (61-cm) length of yellow yarn to the bottom of the rubberband mouth. Drop the yarn down through the tube holder so that it hangs out. To make the sun puppet look like it is talking, just pull on the end of the yarn.

What does your sun want to say?

7)

Make this fan to cool you off on those hot summer days.

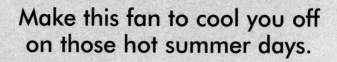

Plate Fan

Here is what you need:

two 9-inch (23 cm) paper plates

markers in several bright colors

tissue paper in several bright colors

plastic tub for mixing

water

white glue

scissors

paintbrush

tongue depressor

yarn

newspaper to work on

Here is what you do:

1 Use the markers to make areas of bright color on the front of one plate and the back of the other.

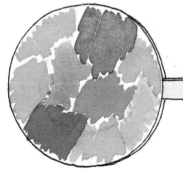

2 Glue the two plates together with the colors showing on the outside and the end of the tongue depressor forming a handle between them.

8)

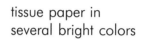

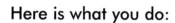

3 Cut flowers from different colored tissue paper. Cut a center for each flower from a contrasting color. Cut some green tissue leaves.

4 Mix one part white glue with one part water in the plastic tub. Carefully paint over one side of the fan with the watery glue to blend the colors. Do not use too much glue on the surface or the colors will become smeared and muddy. Stick some tissue flowers and leaves on the wet surface. Gently cover the tissue flowers and leaves with more watery glue. Let the fan dry. Then turn it over and do the same thing on the other side.

5 Cover the handle with glue, then wrap it in yarn.

What a pretty way to stir up a breeze!

This little mouse will keep your sunglasses safe when you're not using them.

Mouse Sunglasses Case

Here is what you need:

 old necktie

 plastic wrap

 yarn

 scissors

two large and one medium-size pom-poms

 white glue

 sticky Velcro dots fastener

clamp clothespins

two wiggle eyes

Here is what you do:

1 Cut a 9-inch (23-cm) long piece using the wide end of the necktie. (Don't include the point of the tie when you measure.) Carefully cut the tag off the back of the tie. If the front of the tie is sewn to the back of the tie, cut the threads. If the seam of the tie is unraveling, glue it back together. Use a small amount of glue so that you do not stain the fabric. Slip some plastic wrap behind the seam to keep the glue from soaking through the front of the tie.

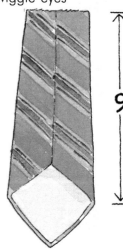

9"

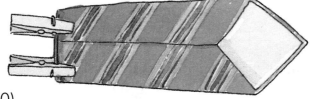

2 Fold the cut opening of the tie inside itself and glue it together. Use clamp clothespins to hold the seam in place until the glue has dried.

10)

3 Stick a Velcro dot on the inside point of the tie. Fold the point over to close the top. Put the other dot on the tie in a position so that the Velcro dots will meet when the case is closed.

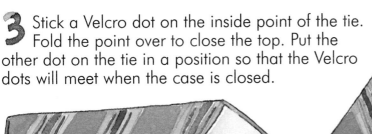

4 Turn the case into a mouse by gluing a large pom-pom ear on each side of the top of the case above the closed point. Glue two wiggle eyes below the ears. Cut two, 3-inch (8-cm) long pieces of yarn. Knot the yarn in the middle, then fray the ends to look like whiskers. Glue the whiskers on the tip of the point with a pom-pom nose glued over the knot in the center.

You might want to make your sunglasses case to look like a different animal. Use your own ideas to make your favorite critter.

11)

Collect farewell messages from your school friends and hello messages from your new camp friends.

Greeting Card Autograph Book

Here is what you need:

 ten or more old greeting cards

 hole punch

 scissors

 cereal box cardboard

marker

pencil

ribbon

Here is what you do:

1 Draw a simple shape on the box cardboard to use as a pattern for the pages of your book. A heart, circle, or flower would work well. The shape should be small enough to fit on the greeting cards. Cut the shape out.

2 Trace the shape on the front of the card you wish to use for a cover for the book. Cut the shape out.

12)

3 Trace the shape on the back of the picture on the front of all the other greeting cards. The back will be the front of the page in your book so that people can write a message that will show well. The greeting card pictures will appear across from each page when the book is tied together. Cut all the shapes out.

4 Stack all the pages together with the cover on the front. Punch two holes through the left edge of the stacked pages. Use the ribbon to tie the pages together loosely so that they will turn easily.

Write on the front of the book with a marker. You could write "Fourth Grade" or the name of your camp or just "My Friends" and the year. Think about making another book next year so that you will someday have a collection to help you remember those special times in your life.

June, and the start of summer, is the most popular time for weddings.

Play Wedding Veil

Here is what you need:

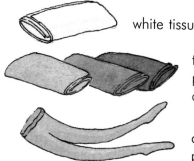

white tissue paper

tissue or crepe paper in your choice of colors

old pair of pantyhose

scissors

stapler

Here is what you do:

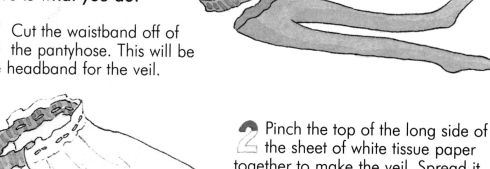

1 Cut the waistband off of the pantyhose. This will be the headband for the veil.

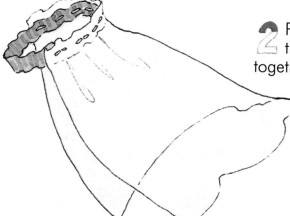

2 Pinch the top of the long side of the sheet of white tissue paper together to make the veil. Spread it out to fit and staple it along one half of the headband. The ends of the staples should be on the outside of the veil so that they will not catch your hair if they do not close completely.

3 Cut 3-inch (8-cm) circles from the colored tissue paper to make flowers. Cut 2-inch (5-cm) squares of tissue to make a center for each flower. Place a square in the center of each circle and pinch the center together to form a flower. Staple the flowers all the way around the headband (half of them will be on top of the white tissue veil). Again, make sure that the staple closes on the outside of the headband.

Here comes the bride!

15)

This key chain is made extra special by putting a picture of you in it. What a great gift to make for Father's Day.

Photo Key Chain

Here is what you need:

 pry-off bottle cap

 scrap of clear Con-Tac paper

 pencil

 scissors

 white glue

 masking tape

 felt scrap

 paper clip

 notebook ring

 small face photo of you

 Styrofoam tray

Here is what you do:

1. Carefully trace around your face in the photo, using the bottom of the bottle cap as a pattern. Cut the traced circle on the photo out. Trim it to fit inside the bottle cap. Cover the photo with clear Con-Tac paper to protect it and trim the excess Con-Tac paper away. Glue the photo inside the bottle cap.

16)

2 Cover the back of the bottle cap with masking tape. Glue a paper clip to the back of the cap with the end sticking up over the top of the photo in front. Cover the bottom of the paper clip with masking tape. Cut a circle of felt to cover the back of the cap. Glue it on the back of the cap to cover the bottom of the paper clip. Let the project dry on a Styrofoam tray.

3 Open the notebook ring and slip one end through the paper clip. Close the notebook ring.

What a nice surprise for your dad!

17)

Show your patriotic spirit by wearing this Uncle Sam mask on the Fourth of July.

Uncle Sam Mask

Here is what you need:

 9-inch (23-cm) paper plate

 red, white, and blue construction paper

 sticker stars

 fiberfill

 white glue

 scissors

 stapler

Here is what you do:

1 Cut the center out of the paper plate, so that you are left with just the rim.

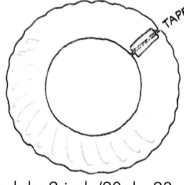

TAPE

2 Cut an 8-inch by 9-inch (20- by 23-cm) piece of blue construction paper for the hat. Cut a 2-inch by 12-inch (5- by 30-cm) blue rectangle for the brim of the hat. Glue the brim across the bottom of one of the shorter sides of the hat piece.

18)

3 Cut a band and stripes for the hat from the red and white paper. Arrange them in a way you like, then glue them in place. Finish the hat by decorating it with sticker stars.

4 Glue a fiberfill beard around half of the plate rim. Staple the hat to the plate rim above the beard.

BACKSIDE

5 Cut a paper band that will be just long enough to fit around your head when attached to each side of the plate rim behind the hat. Staple the band to the plate rim.

Have a glorious Fourth of July!

19)

This happy little firecracker will be around to share more than one Fourth of July with you.

Firecracker Finger Puppet

Here is what you need:

 reddish color coin wrapper

 two wiggle eyes

 sticker stars

 red marker

small bubble wrap

two 12-inch (30-cm) sparkle stems

 small red pom-pom

 scissors

 white glue

Here is what you do:

1 Cut the two sparkle stems in half. Glue the ends of the four pieces inside one end of the coin wrapper. Let the glue dry, then fan the stems out to look like an exploding firecracker.

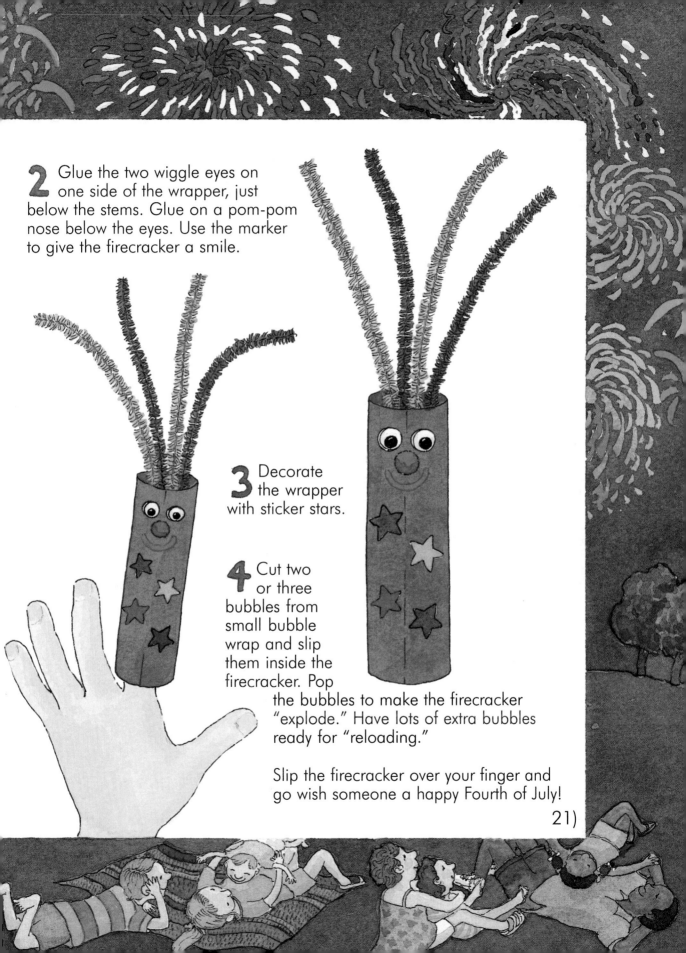

2 Glue the two wiggle eyes on one side of the wrapper, just below the stems. Glue on a pom-pom nose below the eyes. Use the marker to give the firecracker a smile.

3 Decorate the wrapper with sticker stars.

4 Cut two or three bubbles from small bubble wrap and slip them inside the firecracker. Pop the bubbles to make the firecracker "explode." Have lots of extra bubbles ready for "reloading."

Slip the firecracker over your finger and go wish someone a happy Fourth of July!

21)

Bubble blowing is a favorite warm-weather activity.

Bubble Machine

Here is what you need:

 8 oz. (227g) plastic margarine tub with lid

 flexi-straw

hole punch

 black permanent marker

 self-stick stickers

liquid dish soap or detergent

Here is what you do:

1 Punch a hole in the top edge of the plastic margarine tub. Punch another hole in the edge of its lid. Replace the lid, positioning the hole in the lid on the opposite side from the hole in the tub.

2 Write "The Bubble Machine" on the top of the lid with the marker.

3 Decorate around the tub with stickers.

4 Slide the straw into the hole in the side of the tub, bent end first.

5 To use the bubble machine, open the lid and put in a squirt of liquid dish soap. Fill the tub halfway full with water. Put the lid on and blow through the straw. You will be rewarded with a cascade of bubbles pouring out through the hole in the lid.

Try blowing very slowly to see how big a bubble you can make.

Summertime means lots of picnics. Make this sit-upon to use when the ground is damp.

Sit-Upon

Here is what you need:

10 double sheets of newspaper

clear trash bag

clear packing tape

scissors

wrapping paper in a pretty pattern

Here is what you do:

1 Fold one of the double sheets of newspaper into a triangle and then trim off one end so that when you open the newspaper it is shaped like a square. Do this with all ten sheets of paper. Stack the squares.

CUT HERE

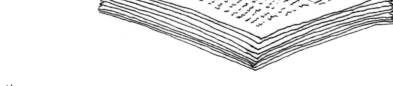

24)

2 Cover the stack of newspaper with wrapping paper, wrapping the stack of squares in the paper and taping the ends just as you would a present. This will be your mat to sit on.

3 Put the mat into one corner of the bottom of the clear trash bag. Trim the top part of the bag off about 6 inches (15 cm) above the mat. Fold the excess bag at the top and one side of the mat over to make the bag cover the square exactly. Use packing tape to hold the bag in place and seal any open seams to make it waterproof.

A sit-upon is just what you need for picnics and camping trips.

This little ant is so cute, you may even want to invite it to your next picnic.

Bead Ant Pin

Here is what you need:

  three small wooden beads

 black paint

paintbrush

 two tiny wiggle eyes

 brown pipe cleaner

 pin backing

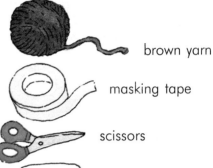 brown yarn

masking tape

scissors

 white glue

Here is what you do:

1 Paint the beads black and let them dry.

2 Double the pipe cleaner and stick the folded end in glue. String the three beads on the glued end. Cut the excess pipe cleaner ends off leaving about ½ inch (1 cm) sticking out one end of the row of beads.

26)

3 Bend the pipe cleaner ends up to form an antennae for the ant.

4 Glue two wiggle eyes under the antennae.

5 Cut three, 1-inch (2.5-cm) pieces of yarn. Glue them to the bottom of the center bead of the ant's body to form the legs.

6 Wrap the base of the pin backing in masking tape to help it stick to the ant. Glue the pin backing over the legs on the center bead of the ant.

Ants live in big colonies. Why not make a friend for this one and wear them as scatter pins?

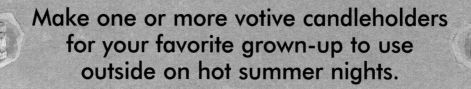

Make one or more votive candleholders for your favorite grown-up to use outside on hot summer nights.

Seashell Candleholder

Here is what you need:

two small baby food jars, one with a lid

masking tape

white glue

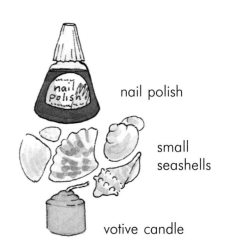
nail polish

small seashells

votive candle

Here is what you do:

1 Paint around the edge of the lid with nail polish.

2 Fill one jar with pretty seashells and put on the lid.

3 Cover the top of the lid and the bottom of the second jar with masking tape to create a better gluing surface. Glue the empty jar on top of the jar of seashells.

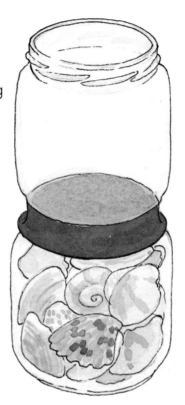

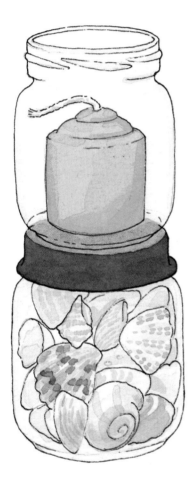

 Put the candle in the top jar.

You might want to fill the bottom jar of your candleholder with some other natural material such as stones. You can also fill it with flowers with a little water. If you do this, you will need to change the contents in a day or two.

Here is a nice way to use some of the seashells you bring home from the beach.

Seashell Locket

Here is what you need:

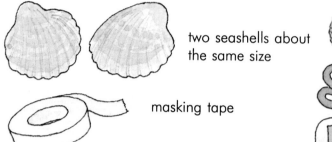

two seashells about the same size

masking tape

scrap of colored tissue paper

yarn

scissors

white glue

small photograph

Here is what you do:

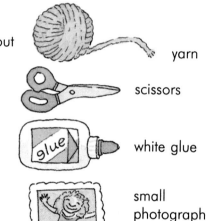

1 Hold the two shells together with the insides facing each other to form a locket. Use masking tape to make a loose hinge between the two shells at the narrow end. Make sure the shells will open and close easily.

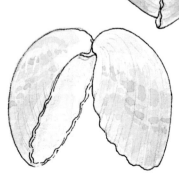

30)

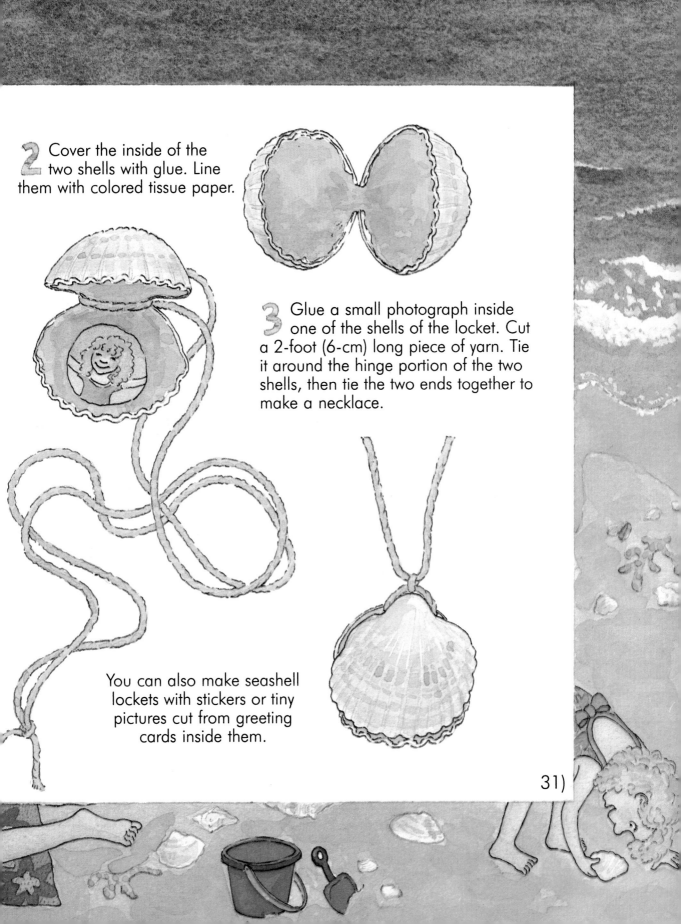

2 Cover the inside of the two shells with glue. Line them with colored tissue paper.

3 Glue a small photograph inside one of the shells of the locket. Cut a 2-foot (6-cm) long piece of yarn. Tie it around the hinge portion of the two shells, then tie the two ends together to make a necklace.

You can also make seashell lockets with stickers or tiny pictures cut from greeting cards inside them.

31)

Swimming Fish Box

Here is what you need:

 box with acetate cover, such as the type stationery comes in

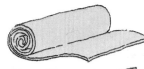 craft foam or flat packing foam

 bubble wrap

markers

 stapler

scissors

 facial tissue

Here is what you do:

1 Use the markers to color an ocean scene on the bottom of the box.

32)

2 Cut a piece of bubble wrap to cover the bottom and sides of the inside box. Staple the bubble wrap in place over the ocean scene.

3 Cut 1-inch (2.5-cm) long fish from the craft foam. If you do not have two or three different colors of foam, you may want to add some color or detail with the markers. Make at least ten fish.

4 Put the fish inside the box and put the lid on. To make the fish swim around inside the box, rub the plastic lid with a facial tissue. Rubbing your fingers across the lid can work too. The static electricity that you create causes the fish to move around the ocean scene.

You might want to add some other sea creatures to your ocean scene. Maybe a wavy eel or sea turtle?

Some people do not like to touch fish, but this fish is fun to feel.

Squishy Fish

Here is what you need:

- construction paper in two colors
- black and white construction paper
- rick-rack or other trim
- yarn

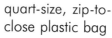
- quart-size, zip-to-close plastic bag
- pencil

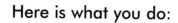
- sequins

- hair gel, clear or colored
- cereal box cardboard

- scissors

- masking tape

- white glue
- stapler

Here is what you do:

1 Squeeze enough hair gel into the bag to fill it when it is lying flat. Add lots of pretty sequins to the gel. Zip the bag almost completely shut, then work any air bubbles in the gel up to the opening and out of the bag.

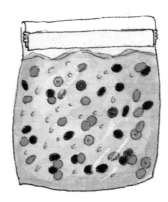

2 Completely seal the bag. Fold the sealed end over and tape it down with masking tape.

3 Fold a piece of 9-inch by 12-inch (23- by 30-cm) construction paper in half to get a piece of paper that is 6 by 9 inches. (15- by 23-cm).

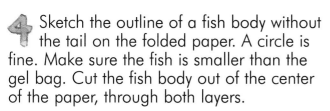

4 Sketch the outline of a fish body without the tail on the folded paper. A circle is fine. Make sure the fish is smaller than the gel bag. Cut the fish body out of the center of the paper, through both layers.

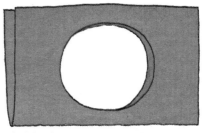

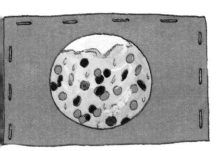

5 Holding the folded paper with the opening at the top, place the gel bag between the folds, with the taped top of the bag at the top open end of the paper. Staple the folded paper shut through the portion of the gel bag above the opening only. (If you staple through the gel bag itself, you will cause it to leak.) Staple the sides of the paper fold shut, also.

6 Cut a 1- by 9-inch (2.5- by 23-cm) strip of cardboard. Staple it across the back of the top opening of the paper for support.

7 Cut a paper tail for the fish and glue it on one side of the fish body.

8 Put a small piece of masking tape on the other end of the fish body. Make an eye for the fish using the black and white construction paper. Stick the eye on the masking tape on the fish body.

9 Cut the rick-rack or trim to glue around the edges of the paper to cover the staples.

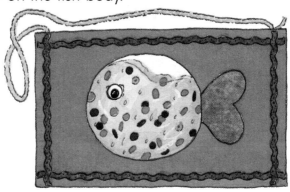

10 Cut a hanger for the fish from yarn and staple an end to each side of the cardboard support at the back of the project.

When you are not squishing your fish, you can hang it in a sunny window for the light to shine through.

35)

Flashing Lighthouse Puppet

Here is what you need:

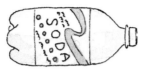 clear plastic 2-quart (2-liter) soda bottle

 scissors

 brown marker

 gray and black construction paper

 white glue

 cellophane tape

 flashlight

black permanent marker

Here is what you do:

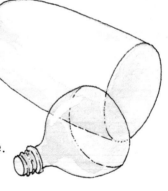

1 Cut the top off the bottle where it starts to go in to form the spout. Turn the bottle over to form the lighthouse.

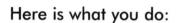

2 Cut a piece of gray paper to cover the lighthouse, leaving the bumpy bottom portion of the bottle (now the top of the lighthouse) uncovered for the light to shine through. Wrap the paper around the bottle and use tape to hold it in place.

3 Use the brown marker to draw a stone pattern on the gray paper.

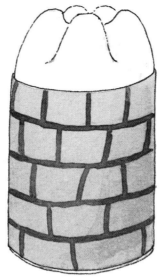

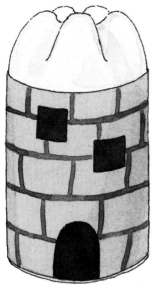

4 Cut windows and a door from the black paper and glue them in place.

5 Use the black marker to draw window bars between the bumps at the top of the lighthouse.

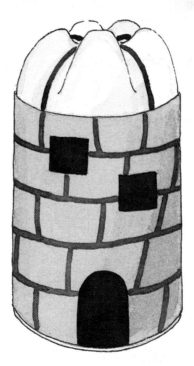

To use the lighthouse puppet, slip the flashlight inside the lighthouse and flash a warning to incoming ships on a dark night.

37)

These little float toys are great for playing in the water on hot summer days.

Cork Float Toys

Here is what you need:

 cork

 two thumbtacks

 white paper

 clear packing tape

 scissors

 markers

Here is what you do:

1 Ask an adult to cut a deep ½-inch (1-cm) long slit in the side of the cork.

2 On the white paper, draw a small picture of something you might find in the water. You could draw some sort of boat or a water animal like a duck. Draw a tab on the bottom of the picture just wide enough to slip into the slit of the cork.

38)

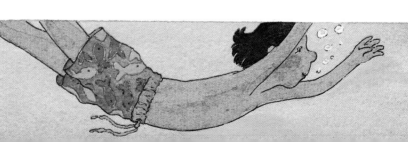

3 Cut out the picture, with the tab. Cover both sides of the picture with clear packing tape to make it waterproof. Cut the picture out again, this time out of the clear tape.

4 Put the picture tab into the slit in the cork.

5 Put a thumbtack on each side of the bottom of the cork below the picture to help keep the cork balanced in the water. (You may need to adjust the thumbtacks to get your toy to float in an upright position.)

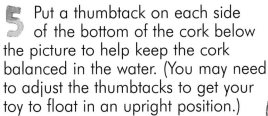

How about making
a fleet of floating toys
and having a race?

Make this boat, complete with passengers, to add to your fun in the water.

Bottle Boat and Cork Passengers

Here is what you need:

 small plastic laundry product jug with handle

 three or more corks

 plastic straw

 Styrofoam tray

 scissors

 black permanent marker

Here is what you do:

1 Cut all the way around the base of the jug about 2½ to 3 inches (6 to 8 cm) up from the bottom. Remove the top portion from the bottle by cutting through the handle, leaving about 3 inches (8 cm) of handle sticking up from the bottle.

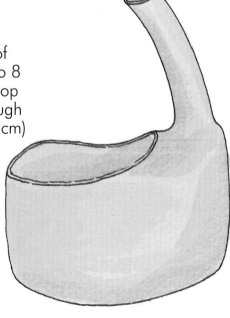

2 Cut a 5- by 5-inch (13- by 13-cm) piece of Styrofoam for the sail. Cut a slit through the top and the bottom center part of the sail. Put the straw through the hollow handle to make a mast for the sail. Slip the sail onto the straw mast through the slits.

S.S. KATHY

3 Use the corks to make passengers for the boat. Draw a face and other details on each cork with the permanent marker. If you decide to name your boat you can write the name on the side with the marker.

Do not worry about an occasional spill. All of the passengers in the boat are very good floaters!

S.S. KATHY

41)

Being near water often means being near lots of seagulls.

Seagull and Fish Puppet

Here is what you need:

two old white socks

clamp clothespin

pipe cleaner

hole punch

scissors

paintbrush

16-ounce plastic soda bottle

orange poster paint

white glue

aluminum foil

black permanent marker

Here is what you do:

1 Cut the top of the plastic bottle about 1 inch (2.5 cm) below where it starts to bend in to form the top.

2 For the beak of the seagull, paint the clothespin orange and let it dry.

3 Thread the pipe cleaner through the curled wire in the clamp clothespin. Punch a hole in each side of the bottom part of the bottle top. Push the clothespin up through the bottle top so that the end sticks out and the two sides that you pinch are still inside the bottle. Thread the two ends of the pipe cleaner through the holes in each side of the bottle to hold the clothespin in place.

42)

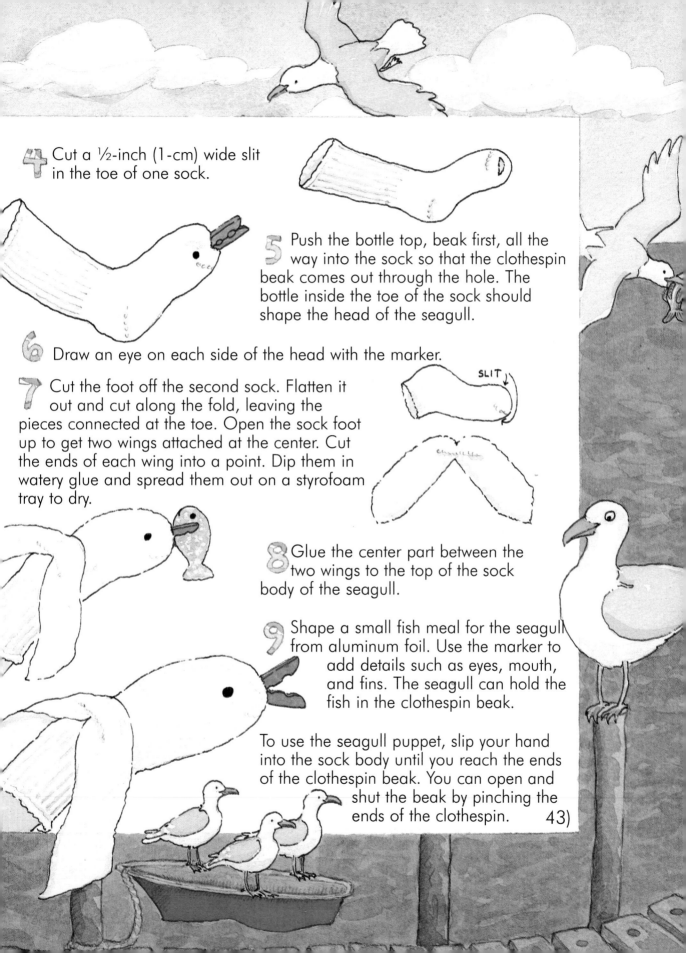

4 Cut a ½-inch (1-cm) wide slit in the toe of one sock.

5 Push the bottle top, beak first, all the way into the sock so that the clothespin beak comes out through the hole. The bottle inside the toe of the sock should shape the head of the seagull.

6 Draw an eye on each side of the head with the marker.

7 Cut the foot off the second sock. Flatten it out and cut along the fold, leaving the pieces connected at the toe. Open the sock foot up to get two wings attached at the center. Cut the ends of each wing into a point. Dip them in watery glue and spread them out on a styrofoam tray to dry.

SLIT

8 Glue the center part between the two wings to the top of the sock body of the seagull.

9 Shape a small fish meal for the seagull from aluminum foil. Use the marker to add details such as eyes, mouth, and fins. The seagull can hold the fish in the clothespin beak.

To use the seagull puppet, slip your hand into the sock body until you reach the ends of the clothespin beak. You can open and shut the beak by pinching the ends of the clothespin.   43)

Jar Water Carafe and Glass

Here is what you need:

two jars, a small one with a rim that will just fit inside a larger one (a large baby food jar and a 25-ounce-size applesauce jar seem to work well together)

 nail polish

Here is what you do:

1 Find a small jar with a rim that just fits inside the larger jar. The small jar will be the water glass and the larger jar will be the water holder. Wash the jars in hot, soapy water to clean them, and remove the labels completely.

44)

Use nail polish to decorate the outside of the large jar.

Fill the large jar with ice water before you go to bed and put the smaller jar over the large jar for a top. If you wake up in the night feeling hot and thirsty, just take the top jar off the water and use it for a glass. Pour yourself a nice cool drink!

Long ago girls and women wore big sunbonnets to protect themselves from the hot summer sun.

Sunbonnet Girl
Door Hanging

Here is what you need:

old shirt with a collar

yarn in a hair color

markers

pretty ribbon

6-inch (15-cm) paper bowl

stapler

white glue

scissors

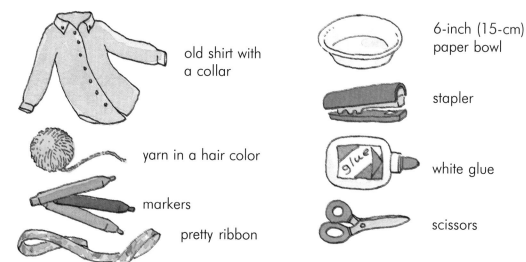

Here is what you do:

1 Cut the collar off the shirt below the neckband. This will be the sunbonnet. Staple the neckband around the inside of the bowl. Fold the collar back toward the bottom of the bowl so that the collar frames the bottom of the bowl like a bonnet.

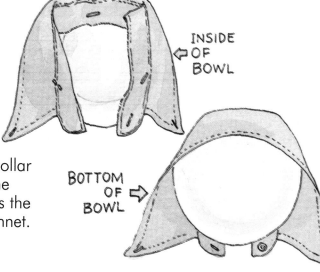

INSIDE OF BOWL

BOTTOM OF BOWL

2 Use the markers to draw a face on the bottom of the bowl.

3 Cut bits of yarn and glue them around the face for hair.

4 Make a pretty ribbon bow. Staple the bow at the bottom of the face to look like the tied strings of the bonnet.

5 Cut a 12-inch (30-cm) long piece of ribbon. Staple the two ends of the ribbon to the back top of the face to form a hanger.

Hang this pretty little sunbonnet girl up for everyone to admire.

47)

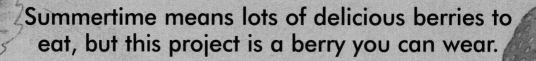

Summertime means lots of delicious berries to eat, but this project is a berry you can wear.

Strawberry Necklace

Here is what you need:

 walnut

 red nail polish

 green felt scrap

 plastic lid for drying

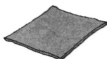 green yarn

scissors

 white glue

Here is what you do:

1 Paint the walnut with red nail polish to make it look like a strawberry. Let it dry on the plastic lid. You may want to paint one side at a time to make sure you get a nice even finish all over.

2 Cut a pointy top leaf for the strawberry from the green felt.

3 Cut a 2-foot (61-cm) long piece of yarn for the necklace. Cut a slit in the center of the strawberry leaf. Slip the two ends of the yarn through the slit.

4 Glue the leaf with yarn to the flatter end of the walnut, with the yarn ends between the felt leaf and the walnut.

You could make several walnut strawberries without a yarn hanger. They are lots of fun to use for play food and look very pretty displayed in a plastic berry basket.

49)

This project can only be done on a hot day.

Melted Crayon Jars

Here is what you need:

 jar

 old crayons in bright colors

 scissors

 aluminum foil

 ribbon

Here is what you do:

1 Choose two or three different crayons in colors that look well together. Break the crayons into small pieces. If you use a large jar, you will need more crayons than if your jar is small. (Three crayons will cover a baby food jar.)

2 Tear off a square of aluminum foil. Place the foil outside in hot, direct sunlight. Sprinkle the crayons on the foil.

Lemonad
15¢/cup

50)

3 The crayons will melt quickly, so be ready with your jar. Do not wait until the crayons are completely melted or they will blend together to make a muddy color. When they have melted, but still have some lumps in them, roll the jar around in the melted crayons to coat it. When you are happy with the design on the jar, take it to a cool place. The crayon will harden and set almost immediately.

4 Tie a bow around the neck of the jar.

These jars are both pretty and useful containers for such things as flowers, pencils, and odds and ends. They are fun and easy to make and each one is different. Remember to keep your finished jars out of direct sunlight or the crayon coating will melt again.

51)

The earth is full of creepy, crawly things to watch on lazy summer days.

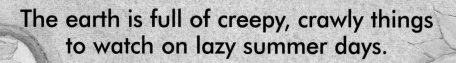

Friendly Earthworm Puppet

Here is what you need:

plastic cup

flexi-straw

green construction paper

masking tape

brown tissue paper

white glue

two tiny wiggle eyes

Styrofoam tray for drying

plastic margarine tub for mixing

water

paintbrush

pencil

scissors

Here is what you do:

1 Mix one part glue with one part water in the plastic tub.

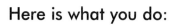

2 Cut a 2-inch (5-cm) wide strip of brown tissue paper about as long as your straw.

3 Paint the tissue paper with the watery glue. Roll the gluey paper around the straw to cover it. Carefully slide the wet tissue up on the straw towards the bent end so that it crumples together to form the segments of the worm. Do this until half the straw is exposed. Pinch the tissue paper over the open end of the straw to make the head of the worm.

4 Glue two tiny wiggle eyes on the head. Let it dry on a Styrofoam tray.

5 Use the pencil to poke a hole in the bottom of the cup. Cover the sides of the cup with strips of masking tape to create a better gluing surface.

6 Trace your hand on the green paper. Cut out three or four green hand shapes. Glue the hands around the cup with the fingers sticking up over the rim of the cup to form grass. You may need to use masking tape to hold the hands in place while the glue dries.

7 Push the uncovered end of the straw down into the hole in the bottom of the cup so that the worm is hidden down in the cup.

Push on the straw sticking out the bottom of the cup to make the worm pop up out of the grass and take a look around.

53)

Summertime means vacations. Make these beautiful note cards to use when writing to your friends who are traveling or when you are away from home.

Brown Bag Note Card

Here is what you need:

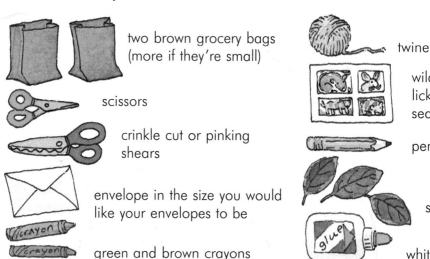

two brown grocery bags (more if they're small)

scissors

crinkle cut or pinking shears

envelope in the size you would like your envelopes to be

green and brown crayons

twine

wildlife or other lick-and-stick seals

pencil

small leaves

white glue

Here is what you do:

1 Cut up the seam of a grocery bag and cut out the bottom of the bag so that you have a flat piece of brown paper. You will need to cut at least two grocery bags and maybe more. You can cut the bags all at once or cut them as you need them.

54)

2 Carefully unglue the seams of the envelope you have chosen and spread it out flat to use as a pattern. Trace around the envelope on the grocery bag paper. Cut out the envelope outline. Fold the envelope that you have cut from the bag at exactly the same places as your envelope pattern was folded. Glue the seams together, leaving the top open. Make at least four envelopes.

3 Make folding note cards to fit inside of each envelope by cutting them from the brown paper. To decorate each note card, put two or three leaves under the front of the card with the vein side of each leaf up, and use a crayon to make a rubbing of the leaves on the card. You can use more than one color to make the rubbing. You might want to experiment with the way you arrange the leaves and the colors you use. Do this on some scrap pieces from the cut bags. If you wish, give the note cards a crinkle edge using pinking shears or crinkle cut scissors.

4 To make the envelopes close, moisten only the top half of the seal and stick it at the point of the flap of the envelope. To close the envelope, the bottom half of the seal can be moistened and stuck to the envelope.

If you plan to give a set of cards away as a gift, stack the note cards and envelopes and tie them together with twine.

55)

Snakes like to come out and sunbathe in the summertime.

Endless Designs Snakes

Here is what you need:

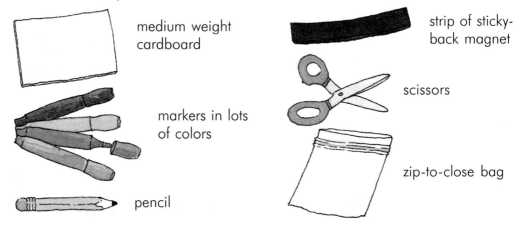

medium weight cardboard

markers in lots of colors

pencil

strip of sticky-back magnet

scissors

zip-to-close bag

Here is what you do:

1 Use the pencil to draw a 10-inch long (25-cm) snake on the cardboard.

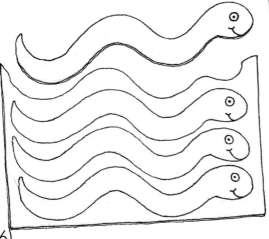

2 Cut the snake out. Use the snake as a pattern to make three more snakes that are all identical.

3 Cut the first snake into four equal sections. Use the sections as a pattern to help you cut the other three snakes exactly the same way.

4 Color a wild design on each section of the snakes. Add a mouth and eye to the head section of each snake.

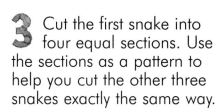

5 Put a piece of sticky-back magnet on the back of each snake section. Store the snake pieces in a zip-to-close bag.

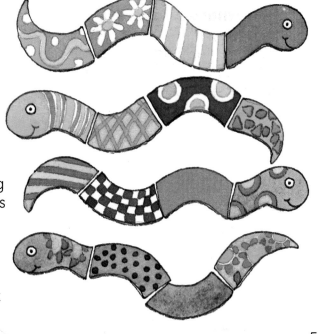

You can design an endless number of snakes by arranging one of each of the four sections of the snake together on your refrigerator. Designer snakes are fun to play with on a long car trip. Just bring along an old metal cookie sheet to stick the pieces to.

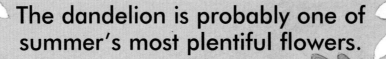

The dandelion is probably one of summer's most plentiful flowers.

Dandelion Corsage

Here is what you need:

yellow and white yarn

green felt

three green 6-inch
(15-cm) pipe cleaners

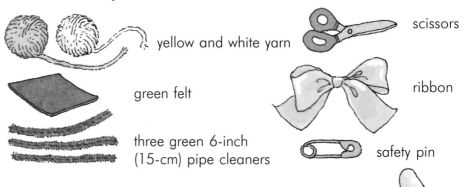

scissors

ribbon

safety pin

Here is what you do:

1 To make a dandelion, wrap yellow
yarn around your hand ten times
and cut the yarn.

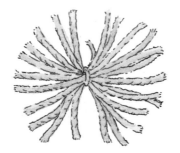

2 Slip the wound yarn off your hand. Tie it
together in the center with another piece
of yellow yarn. Trim the yarn on each side of
the center to about 1 inch (2.5 cm) long.

3 Fray all of the yarn so that it looks
like a fluffy dandelion. To do this,
just unwind the fibers that make up each
strand of yarn.

4 Hook a 6-inch (15-cm) long pipe cleaner through the yarn that holds the flower together at the center. Fold the end over the yarn to hold the pipe cleaner in place to form a stem for the flower.

5 Cut a 1½-inch (4-cm) circle of green felt. Cut little points around the outside of the circle. Cut a small slit in the center of the circle. Slide the circle up the stem of the dandelion to form the green cup of the flower.

6 Make three dandelions. If you want one of the dandelions to look like it has gone to seed, use white yarn instead of yellow yarn.

7 Cut two long, pointy dandelion leaves from the green felt. Cut a small slit in the bottom of each leaf. Slide the leaves up the stems of all three dande-lions until they are sticking up behind the flowers.

8 Tie a pretty ribbon bow around the flowers. Pin a safety pin to the back of the ribbon so that the flowers can be worn as a corsage.

urprise your mom with this pretty ouquet that will last for many immers to come.

59)

Decorated Flowerpot

Here is what you need:

clay flowerpot

green pipe cleaners and four pipe cleaners in bright colors

small stretchy plastic net bag such as toys or produce come in

scissors

Here is what you do:

1 Put the clay pot in the net bag so that the pot is covered by the net. Trim off the extra net at the top of the bag.

60)

2 Decorate around the pot with pipe cleaner flowers. Weave the green stems into the net, spacing them evenly around the pot. Add green pipe cleaner leaves, by wrapping them around the bottom of each stem. Shape four different color pipe cleaner flowers. Wrap the top of each stem around the center of a flower to hold it in place.

You might want to decorate your pot with a different pipe cleaner picture.

Have you ever tried to catch fireflies on a hot summer night?

Flashing Fireflies

Here is what you need:

 two 9-inch (23-cm) paper plates

 paper fastener

 black and brown poster paint

paintbrush

white glue

 gold glitter

clear tape

 lots of tiny wiggle eyes

hole punch

newspaper to work on

Here is what you do:

1 Punch about twenty-four holes all over one of the paper plates, avoiding about an inch (2.5 cm) around the very center of the plate. To punch holes in the middle section, you will need to fold the plate without creasing it and punch two holes at a time.

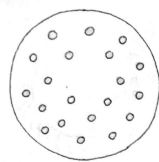

2 Paint the eating side of both paper plates black.

62)

3 Put the plate with the holes on top of the other plate. Hook them together at the center with a paper fastener. Squeeze a drop of glue through each hole. Remove the top plate and cover each dot of glue on the bottom plate with gold glitter. Let the glue dry completely before putting the two plates back together.

←BOTTOM PLATE→

TOP PLATE

4 Use the brown paint to paint a ½-inch (1-cm) firefly body over each hole in the top plate. The hole should be at the back of each firefly.

5 Glue a tiny wiggle eye to the front of each firefly.

6 Make wings for each firefly by twisting a small piece of clear tape at the center and pressing it on the body. When the glue and paint have dried completely, put the plates back together with the paper fastener.

To make the fireflies "flash," line the holes up with the gold glitter dots on the back plate. When you turn the plate slightly to one side, the back of each firefly will turn black. Turn the plate back and forth to make the sparkle come and go.

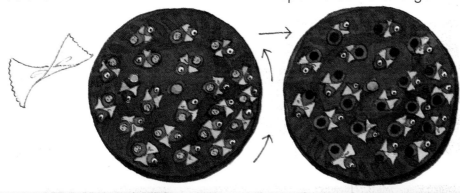

63)

About the Author and Artist

Twenty years as a teacher and director of nursery school programs in Oneida, New York, have given Kathy Ross extensive experience in guiding children through craft projects. A collector of teddy bears and paper dolls, her craft projects have frequently appeared in *Highlights* magazine. She is the author of The Millbrook Press's *Holiday Crafts for Kids* series, including the *Crafts for Kids Who Are Wild About* series, as well as the fall, winter, and spring volumes of this *Crafts for All Seasons*. She has also written *Gifts to Make for Your Favorite Grown-ups*, *Crafts From Your Favorite Fairy Tales* and *Crafts for Kids Who Are Wild About the Wild*.

Vicky Enright is an illustrator living in Andover, Massachusetts, with a small son, two huge labrador retriever dogs, and her husband. To date, she has utilized her talents as a calligrapher, a wallpaper designer, and a greeting card artist. Her first book was *Crafts From Your Favorite Fairy Tales* by Kathy Ross. She is the illustrator of the other three season books in this series: *Crafts to Make in the Spring*, *Crafts to Make in the Fall*, and *Crafts to Make in the Winter*.